This is an enchanting book. Page after page, Paula Bonnell's poetry is full of fresh sightings, sure phrasing, and a ⸻ ⸱ity for giving and taking delight. She can also deal subtly with ⸻ touching things, as in "History and a House." John Ciar⸱ ⸱ that so vital a book has received the prize which be⸱

⸻ ⸱ichard Wilbur

Bonnell's voice is low-⸱ ⸱uirky insights that keep these poems fresh and interes⸱ ⸱y for an Unlikeable Sister-in-law" concludes: "Lord, she anno⸱ ⸱s. / But she was ours." "In Praise of Leeks" captures their "fresh chartreuse / a *tendresse* of green." And the scholar who unearths 16th-century theatrical manager Philip Henslowe's list of properties selects from it: "Item: / one cloak for to go invisible."

—Maxine Kumin

Paula Bonnell has a magic touch. Reading *Airs & Voices* in its entirety, we hear a clear, subtle, witty, and authentic voice; and hearing it, we end up charmed. Engagingly, "An Alphabet" and "Some Tax Aspects of Life" have memorable fun with language; "Serving Two Cats" proves Bonnell one of our best cat-watchers since Christopher Smart. Besides these distinctive poems, I'm particularly smitten with "In the Middle of the Air," "Falling Asleep," "Reconstituting Paris," "The Faraway Nearby," "The Island," and more. "The Voices" may be one of the wisest comments on the catastrophe of 9/11 that an American poet has made.

—X. J. Kennedy

# AIRS &
# VOICES

# AIRS & VOICES

*Poems by*

*Paula Bonnell*

Winner of the John Ciardi Prize for Poetry
selected by Mark Jarman

 BkMk Press
University of Missouri-Kansas City

Copyright © 2008 by Paula Bonnell

BkMk Press
University of Missouri-Kansas City
5101 Rockhill Road
Kansas City, Missouri 64110
(816) 235-2558 (voice) / (816) 235-2611 (fax)
www.umkc.edu/bkmk

Cover design: John Martucci
Cover art: Kono Bairei
Associate editor: Michelle Boisseau
Managing editor: Ben Furnish
Assistant Managing Editor: Susan L. Schurman

BkMk Press wishes to thank: Teresa Collins, Chelsea Seguin,
Sandra Meyer, Janet Conner, Christopher Glenn, Emily Iorg,
Elizabeth Gromling.

The John Ciardi Prize for Poetry wishes to thank:
Andrés Rodríguez, Susan Cobin, Lindsey Martin Bowen, Maryfrances
Wagner, Greg Field, Steve Gehrke, Nadine Meyer, Heather Clark.

Previous winners of the John Ciardi Prize for Poetry: *Wayne's College
of Beauty* by David Swanger, selected by Colleen J. McElroy; *The
Portable Famine* by Rane Arroyo, selected by Robin Becker; *Fence
Line* by Curtis Bauer, selected by Christopher Buckley; *Escape Artist*
by Terry Blackhawk, selected by Molly Peacock; *Kentucky Swami* by
Tim Skeen, selected by Michael Burns; *The Resurrection Machine* by
Steve Gehrke, selected by Miller Williams

**Library of Congress Cataloguing-in-Publication Data**

Bonnell, Paula.
    Airs & voices / Paula Bonnell.
    p. cm.
Poetry.
    ISBN 978-1-886157-62-0
I. Title.   II. Title: Airs and voices.
    PS3552.O6355A73 2007
    811'.54--dc22
                    2007045673

This book is set in Century Schoolbook and Trajan Pro type.

# FOREWORD

The voice in *Airs & Voices* by Paula Bonnell is fresh and original. Though the poet never labors to be significant, even the slightest poem lingers in memory. Wallace Stevens's thoughtfulness is present, but so is his playfulness. Kenneth Koch's playfulness is here, but so is his thoughtfulness. Whether speaking as various snowmen in "New Song" or as parts of a household in "Domestic Opera," the poet finds just the right expression for the subject, with a warmth and good humor that are in short supply nowadays. Sometimes the compassion is startling, as in "Elegy for an Unlikeable Sister-in-Law." Yet an austerity can take hold as well. "The Voices" makes us listen again to the things we said in response to 9/11. Finally, to paraphrase the end of one of the most moving poems in *Airs & Voices*, "History and a House," this poetry is "so good. It must have happened before." And yet it all seems brand new.

—Mark Jarman
Final Judge
John Ciardi Prize for Poetry

for my mother
Jean M. Wolfe

working with her as amanuensis and editor
as she wrote her first novel
(begun when she was 85 and completed when she was 91)
helped release this work
to flow through me

# CONTENTS

## (1)

## (2)

(3)

(1)

# DAWN CHORUS

Before the sun
lifts its fireball over the harbor,
while it is still blazing beneath the horizon, it pushes
dim white light into the upper sky. Then
the animals begin to celebrate.
The cats sharpen their claws, the birds stir
and talk it up. To the starlings' gibberish
and the crows' whole notes, the rooster
adds his boogie-woogie cadenza.
On this city block, a dog
cries *Hark!* to resentful neighbors
and I awaken, put a pillow over my eyes
and go back to sleep.

# NEW SONG

I arrive in the Christmas snow.
Yes, assembly is required—compact
it and roll a few simple snowballs.
Once the small arms of those
delible irregular spheres
are blurred and enlarged
by more and more somersaults
to peaceful blobs, you
have the rudiments.
                              In one yard—
*Roll it and pat it and mark it*
*with* B!—I am small; I wear
a sweater the baby has outgrown.
She laughs at me as she crowed at my making.

Down the block, I am tall,
carrot-nosed. I wear
a Boston College knit hat—or
at least, it perches atop
my large bald head, a head
too wide-browed to be
confined in it.

On Mercier Street I am short
and squatty-bodied. For the first
time that I recall I wear
a bunch of wooden cherries
(saved from an old straw hat)
emblazoned on my chest. I am
decorated for my many
deaths, my losses under fire,
the way my arms always look
prosthetic, my lost legs.

I am still but not sullen,
fugitive without fleeing.
And today, even in this painful
dominion of the sun, I smile
crookedly, joying
in my resurrections in
this new year, new century,
my many new lives,
this strange, strange land.

## WORDS OF A MAN
## WHO MADE HIS NAME

I bore the names
of three men:
the protestant, a slaveholder,
my father.
I saw
what I had to do
and did as much of it
as I could.
I leave
the rest of it
to you.

# ELEGY FOR AN UNLIKEABLE
# SISTER-IN-LAW

It's a relief she can't
hector us any more
And she never listened to us
So there's not that sense
of a conversation interrupted
that has been much of the pain
of other deaths we've known.
There is something we are sorry
for in her lifetime which cannot
be improved by this death.
Maybe there was something
we could have done
even if she had done
little else than what she did.
But it's not that we
mourn for. It's all
the connections not made
that her death
seems to confirm.
Let us pray
not to let this death
grave that in stone.
And one more thing.
Lord, she annoyed us.
But she was ours.

# CALENDAR

The days are like doors,
side by side by side.

Sunday: heavy red curtains
pulled aside, cinched.

Monday, patterned with green coins.
Tuesday, yellow ones.

Wednesday: dark navy, near black.
Thursday, plain, again red.

Friday: black.  A frying pan on it.
Saturday, plain red, but taller

than Thursday.
Sunday: the red curtains.

From a distance, the days
and the doors disappear

and the seasons are seen
as rolling hills.  Down

the verdant slope of spring
to the lush bottomlands

of summer, then toiling
up the slope, harvesting,

till November's gray hill
is lit by the red cave

glowing from inside
the hillock of December

The white gleams as January
begins its slope down

to where the year begins.

# IN KÖNIGSBERG

You are ahead of me
perhaps on this island,
perhaps on the north or south bank
or perhaps on the other
side of this bridge that
connects the other island
to this.

I have crossed one bridge
and am willing to cross others
but I hate to retrace
my step or even to
follow myself the same
way a second time

I look forward to seeing
you, to being with you
You are the future
The past is not your
habitat.  Those I remember
(fondly, of course)
were not you

When I imagine
going out of my body
to hover over the city—
its two islands and
gray streets and seven bridges
rainwet, sunlit, stones and
rooftiles silvered—
I can tell
you are here, though
I cannot see
you or hear you,
yet I sense your presence
but beyond which bridge
is unknown,

                    yet
it almost becomes
intuitively obvious
(The bridges are skeletal)
before I return
to inhabit the hairs
and cavities of my body

It is not that you are receding
but that I feel you best
at a distance, knowing
that when we are together
we will be together
and I will find you
if I can cross only
uncrossed bridges

or perhaps, when
I come to that last bridge
and see you lying half-
naked on the barge, sunning
on its smooth planks, and
in the clear water below
the reeds of the river
wavering downstream
reaching toward the bridge where I stand

When I reach that
previously crossed bridge
I will jump off it
and swim in the clear
water, pulling myself
up over the side of the
barge, dripping, and
lie down beside you
close enough to feel
your warmth, to inhale
your characteristic
fragrance

# SKYWRITING

The drogues, pushed by currents, drag the NOPPs through the plankton, the NOPPs busily telling the satellites where they've been, where they're going, and when they'll be home for dinner. Students and scientists write it all down.

The radio voice is talking into the radio mike and onto the radio tapes. The tapes lie silently coiled on their spools. The tapes unwind, writing the voices onto the satellites. The stations wait and point and copy the voice out of the sky, giving it out, broadcast, to listeners.

Faraway stars appear as dots on the outside of the invisible sphere of the night sky. People connect the dots and call them the *Dipper, Orion,* the *Southern Cross*.

The earth revolves within a geodesic net of plotlines which join the points from which stars and satellites arrive and depart. Polygons of emptiness fill the spaces between the lines.

# IN PRAISE OF LEEKS

Their hanks of medusa roots
The green lines in their white parts
The sand and mud they saved,
        pushing up through the earth
Their roundness at the root
Their pointed oval shape
        farther up
The abundance of their greens

Dark green chopped off
Medusa roots off
The core cut out in a
        slanting circular move
Now the knife can bisect
        the pointed oval
and part the leeks
        into stretch-limo parentheses

All their greenness and whiteness
Dramatic outer contrasts
                Split
to reveal a fresh chartreuse
a *tendresse* of green

And how the layers part

And the pleasures of washing
        and washing them
water between all those
        layers, rinsing and rinsing

There is much much more

But it is also possible
to go the other way:
To fall in love first
        with the taste
and the texture

The soups of white parts
The stocks of green parts
The delicious dilemmas
How much of the pale green
    to give to the soup?
How much to the stock?

Or whether to cook the leeks
as a vegetable—
split, then cut lengthwise—
    slowly
    with celery

# THE WATCHERS

It was in the late twentieth century,
the year Beth was born,
that we set out on the boat
to see the whales.
                              For our lunch
I took with us some carrot sticks,
*brandade de morue* thick with garlic,
some bread.  We had coffee
in a thermos.  It was a cold, cold day.

And when we got far
enough from shore—there they were!
Whales rose and
sank, showing flukes
and flanks and markings
white and gray, each one different
so that the crew could tell us names
for most of them and
something of their lives:
where they had been, how old
they were—that sort of thing.
                              This was the last
trip of the season, and the crew
said we were seeing more whales,
*More whales!* than most excursions saw.

Then two adult females and a calf
swam toward the boat.  *The mothers
often get help from other females*, said the crew,
*The calves are curious.*
                              These three
swam very near.  By now they were close beside
the boat and we all rushed to the rail
to see the enormous bodies, just under the water.
The boat tipped down toward the gray threesome,
and we leaned out over the rail.
                              Then they dove down
and came up on the other side.  We rushed
to that rail and the boat tilted
that way!
                  Then the three
stood up in the water and their breath

engulfed us in a fishy oily fog.
*Talk about bad breath!* we exclaimed.
Believe me, it was rank.
We could hardly believe it: we were
almost in their mouths.
                              And now they were down again,
and up on the other side, and standing up
in the water, heads out, to take another look.

The calf saw us.
                              And the mother and her friend
saw that we had come to see them.

# WEATHER REPORT

In the early hours of the morning,
there will be . . .s and ( )s,
followed by a few light !s
and some .s
                    Then
there will be ,s and ;s and .s
for most of the day
and, in the late afternoon
and evening, scattered :s.
By nightfall the ;s and .s will diminish
and ( )s and . . .s will continue
throughout the night. There may
be @!#?&* after midnight.
For tomorrow, there could be ?s.

# A LIST OF PROPERTIES

Stubborn, proud, a little
like the testy schoolmarm
who would correct, correct
and underscore each meritorious
point, having for years been
disappointed in the hope of
a student as brilliant and
punctilious as herself,

she took up books and pen
and limited her scope to
documents extant when
her man was alive.
She did Shakespeare
first, then Ben.
                    *Ah, Ben!*
From all the wealth
of facts—see lengthy
bibliography at the back—
she'd take some single
strand and weave
a scene of well-conjectured
life around it.  No
footnotes.  Let the double-checker
duplicate her labor first.

And when she wrote
of Philip Henslowe and his
loans to playwrights, how
much advanced to this, how
much repaid by that, the careful
books that detailed each expense,
she read a list
of properties and notes
just this:  *Item:*
*one cloak for to go invisible.*

# SERVING TWO CATS

The upstairs cat is fur over clockwork.
The cat downstairs is plush over hydraulic energy.
    Upstairs is tiger;
    Downstairs, tabby.

Both have odd purrs.
The upstairs cat's is transparent,
    no thickness, almost inaudible,
    like layered breathing.
The downstairs cat is a singing boy;
    his purr whistles. Like a harmonica player,
    he uses in and out for double effects.

Upstairs has a squirrel tail.
He arches it toward his shoulder blades
    as if he held a lantern for himself.
Downstairs is so relaxed he's fluid.
He can be picked up and held upside down
    with ease—he is totally confident
    in any position.

Downstairs says *Yes! You are here! I am glad*
    *to see you!*
Upstairs says *Where have you been? What is*
    *this orange-and-white hair?*
    *What is this smell on your hands?*
Downstairs says *Must you go? Stay and commune*
    *with me . . .*
Upstairs assumes the sphinx posture and
    considers riddles.

Soon this week of cat bigamy will be over and
    Katja and Andrew will return.
I reflect on our exchange before they left.
I said, *There's nothing I'd like better*
    *than to serve two cats.*
And Andrew replied,
    *But is it wise to serve two cats?*

# AIR

The music is not over until the chords resolve—
the notes appear and recognize each other
by a nod, a bow, a curtsey—or a wink
and then they change their places by a set
of steps, a link of arms, an intricate
enactment of a figure, and double back
to take it from the top.
                  Why would they
stop unless their pauses made a shimmer
in the sheen of color that they give the air?
Their nameless naming, lightless bright illumination
makes melody and respite and release
until and after all their chords dissolve.

# EARLY LEARNING

Each child, after being warned
of what is hot, after having
learned *blue, red, green,*
and before it learns the alphabet
or the shapes of the fifty states,
is shown pictures of lion,
zebra, elephant, giraffe,
and will be taken to see
any of those animals
kept nearby.

                        She was born in a hard year.
Her father named her *Famine.*
She married a Peace Corps worker
(who paid the bride price of
two sacks of rice, a goat,
a chicken) and they moved here
where ten years of marriage
were followed by a divorce.
                             Our guest
at dinner, she picks up one
of the animal napkin rings, Kenyan
carvings for the tourist trade,
and expatiates on the giraffe.
*This animal is very stupid,*
*a great nuisance,* she says.
*He will not get out of the road.*

# IN THE MIDDLE OF THE AIR

Not soaring like the vulture
or the rough-legged hawk

Nor harrying the marshes
like its northern cousin

Not flying from tree to tree
like the songbirds

Nor flitting from one leafy interior
to another like the warblers

But in a middle distance
at an audible height

where they're their own size
not reduced to images of themselves

Hardworking wingbeats of heavy-bodied geese

They are flying and talking
to each other, exhorting and saying
what they are doing even as they do it
(what's called in my house
*squawking and pretty talking*)

To each other, they announce progress
and effort, determination, encouragement

and I hear passage—sudden
arrival and quick-gradual departure,
passengers of their own flight

This spring evening, coming through the yard,
the sky drenched in dark blue
the air near the grass dimmed

I hear them calling overhead

Not in the distant sky
but in nearby air

and I look up to the housetops
but cannot find the moving V.

Vivid invisible northward honking
above the rooted houses,
the woman standing with key in hand
motionless on the front steps.

# DOMESTIC OPERA

*In order of vocal appearance, blue watering can (BWC), cat, various bonsai. The householder is a mute part, to be played by a dancer.*

BWC:      Blue, I am blue

Cat:      I, I am

Bonsai:      O sun
O water
O darkness
O sun (& *so on, in madrigal*)

BWC:      Water is mine
I give, I give
I am exhausted

Cat:      Here, I am here
Here I am

Bonsai:      Drinking, drinking
Dry, thirsty
Rain, rain, yes, rain
Leaves wet, trembling

BWC:      My stem is long
My tip narrow
I am carried
I am emptied
I am refilled

Cat:      Serve me food
Serve me

Bonsai:      Feeling for light
Feeling the light
Now, now
Glorious
Now

BWC:      I am empty

Cat:              On this windowsill
I   stretch   out,   I   watch

Bonsai:      It is dark
Drying
Resting
Dancing in the wind

# AN ALPHABET

*for Rosario*

To transcribe the secret language in which
we might converse privately, even in crowds,

there must be an alphabet.  I would take
its curves from your eyebrows, long arches,

and its straight legs, the erect slender carriage
of its letters from yours.  The spaces

that fill its closed curves I would fill
with the colors of the imagination.  These

would bleed gently out of the open curves
of such letters as *C* into the surrounding

countryside of the air.  In this way,
moods could be annotated along with meanings.

And there would be a great wardrobe
of diacritical marks for the letters

to clothe themselves in.  A barred *d*,
thus: ð, would paint the clouded *d*,

softened with *th*, in the name *Clada*.
For hair clips and bracelets, the letters

would wear accents and cedillas; for hats,
circumflexes; for scarves, tildes.  And of course

that comfortable somersaulter the schwa
would be one of the letters.  And there

would, as well, be times when the letters
would go plainly into the air, unadorned,

practical, the hip-booted *g* and *q*
wading below the line to catch flashing

creatures as food for the thoughts
we exchanged.  This language would always

be making new words, sometimes several
a day, sometimes only one nuance

in a month.  But it would grow, and
change, and modulate to accommodate

all the joyful, sorrowful, and glorious
mysteries of our lives, each with its own name.

# THANKS

Somewhere there must be a book
that explains the book we are in

Someone is reading the words
that name this flannel, these birds,

this morning opening like a lens
so that we can see, can put away

the dishes washed yesterday, cook
today's applesauce to put into

the refrigerator of tomorrow for
the desserts of the coming week.

Just as some time on the farm
in Vermont, my sister wrote

*Applesauce 1998, Batch 3* on the lid
and put into the freezer

the white plastic cylinder
which, thawed, gave me

day's-end pleasure all
last week so that I, unlike

the woodpecker, beginning his
*rat-a-tat-tat*, could eat

and bless the work of
another, the food of love.

# EVIDENCE

Not accepting the gossip of starlings,
the woodpecker waits until

the red eye of the sun has
cleared the horizon and hangs

at the height of a captive balloon
before he begins the morning's

drill.  I open the window to
try to discover if part of

the tree is dead, or if it's
my house he explores, or

if the telephone pole on the
corner could possibly yield

anything of interest for this
industrious bird and his

pleasant hollow tattoo, but
the noise alarms him

and all I can tell from
his black-and-white flight

is that he came from
somewhere off to the left.

(2)

# BOSTON, POST OFFICE SQUARE

In the small triangle
of Angell Memorial Park,
lindens lift their elbows
in awkward grace,
       a clutch of vegetable umbrellas

Each spring
when the trees
in the neighboring park park
(*Park above. Park below.*),
begin to quicken
these lindens,
         in a suspenseful
chapter, seem to delay

This year—*Oh, bleak!*
One, like an umbrella
in rigor mortis
after a storm,
could not unfold
its green miracle

The caretakers
spirited it away
seemingly in the night
(or more probably
while the oblivion
of work shrouded
the park from the sight
of office workers)

and supplanted it with
the gift of
a new, young
tree, its arms
reaching down in
a smooth slant
without crook or hesitation
eagerly toward the bronze ducks.

# GRESHAM'S LAW

Listen to the mockingbird—
*Per diem, per diem, per diem!*
he says. *Free, free, free!*
And then he reverts
to *Twee, twee, twee—*
*tlee, tlee, tlee.*
It seems it was only
yesterday when he
was satisfied with
*Dietrich! Dietrich!*
and *Drink your tea!*

# FALLING ASLEEP

In the summer, the entry
is through a snowbank:

cool cotton, a drift of
sheets soothe the hot limbs

and let the mind
into the cavern of dreams

In winter, a cocoon
of flannel, wool, and down

contain the
body's warmth

so that the soul
may flow into

gigantic wrinkled
wings, folded around

the body, sticky
in the dark

until the husk splits
and the light leaks in

# HISTORY & A HOUSE

The house is old, built in
the late 1700s.  The time is
our times, circa 1992.
The man on the bed says
*I wonder how many people*
*have had their feet rubbed*
*in this house* and the
man on the floor
understands him to mean
*I wonder how many people*
*have died in this house.*
The reader reading
the account by the one
left alone to tell this tale
understands him to mean
*I wonder how many people*
*have been loved and*
*cared for in this house.*
*And I wonder if any*
*of them were loved*
*enough that the one*
*who cared for them*
*got down to rub their feet.*
Christ washed his apostles'
feet.  And English kings used to
wash the feet of the poor
each year on Maundy Thursday.
Pepys remarks (April 4, 1667)
that the restored Charles did not
wash the poor people's feet
himself; the Bishop
of London did it for him.
History is a large place
housing a few facts, a lot
of inaccurate summaries,
and many conflicting ideas.

But this house near the
sea, enclosed by the dark
and holding lamplight,
pushed by the night winds
and still holding
to its foundation,
flooded with daylight, is
a small, real place,
here. And the foot,
which can feel so
much pain and so
much pleasure and
which does so much work,
thankless, is felt and
held and touched and
helped, here,
where one man is too
tactful to speak his pain
in the knowledge of coming
death, not wanting to
underline the obvious,
and the other cannot
claim out loud the great
love being given him.
He did not say,
but I imagine he thought
*I wonder who lived here before*
*who loved someone enough*
*to make them feel better*
*like this, by touching*
*the humble foot*
*with the important hand?*
*This love is so good,*
*so good. It must*
*have happened before.*

# INTERWOVEN

The innocence of morning—
a cool purity—
has been filtered through
an evening of experience—
dark as charcoal—
itself a product
of burning a fuel, wood,
near a hut in the woods
(fairytale) but the fact is
that the wood itself—
the vitality of trees—
is produced by light.

# DOES *LIKE* COUNT?

This is a fake poem.
It lurks among the
real poems, disguised
in lines, so it can pass.
It's willing to say
things —like, *I just*
*walked through Harvard Yard*
*and heard twelve languages*
*being spoken.* And
to take them back—
because how do I
know? I did hear
a young man say to
his girlfriend
*Like, Asian grandmothers*
*are, like, really*
*independent.* She giggled
in a conspiratorial way.
And I liked the vision
of at least four grandmothers,
high-ranking face cards,
all wild. And it was
written on the T, the way
real poems sometimes are.
But as I said,
this poem isn't real.
It wasn't inspired.
I wrote it on purpose.

I shut my soul into
the medicine cabinet,
where it was imprisoned
behind a mirror.
It was quiet.
I didn't hear it
when I leaned
forward attending
to a pimple or a
hair.  People talk
about this kind of
thing at meetings,
their midnight
trysts with the substance
behind the mirrored
door—how they
couldn't stay away
from it, couldn't get
enough of it.
                    But
the worst part is
that the damned
thing makes its
home in the cabinet
and keeps going
back.  I couldn't
get it to live
inside of me
again, to look
out my eyes,
breathe my breath.
I don't know
whether to accuse
the soul or myself
of this nameless
nameless
crime.

# THE CLARINET

I can
be anything—
a crying baby,
a train, a
*whoop-de-do!*
The wind
in the trees . . .
I articulate
I stutter
I sing
I jubilate
I whirl
I squeal and chortle
I slow
I mourn
I rest

And the rest
of the band
plays
on

You are
almost relieved
I have stopped

But I know

you
are
also
waiting

for my return

# RECONSTITUTING PARIS

To refill the Seine you can borrow enough water
from Pittsburgh, a city that Paris somewhat resembles,
with its many bridges and its soot-blackened stones.

After the water has begun to flow, breezes will
resume and bits of green begin to push out at the tips
of the pollarded trees.

Soon in the drawers at the Polidor, each marked
with the name of a regular patron, the napkins will
turn over, rousing themselves from dreams of soapsuds
and of the first time, newly ironed, they were folded
and placed in a drawer.

Snails will be served, chicken roasted, the cheese
course arrayed on a round wicker tray. There will be
mustard. The skate will be cooked tender and
glistening.

On the Rue du Dragon, the young woman will whip
the curtains in their free-sliding rings across the open
window, hiding the Stradivarius poster from the eyes of
the hotel guest across the street, and streamers of
virtuosic practicing, bravura flights and diligent
scales, will carry out into the evening air.

On the ceiling of the Sorbonne station of
the Métro, the pink and blue signatures gleam in
the restored light.

A cat jumps up and stations itself in the window
of the concierge's quarters.

French is being spoken by all of Paris; even
Americans are exercising their entire faces as
the embouchures of this intense language, theatrical,
re-enacting each emotion it recounts.

Parisian babies, hearing French, suck harder.

*Ça suffit.* Enough water has been added. *Voilà
Paris, tout complet, bien retrouvé.*

# PROVING THE EXISTENCE OF BARCELONA

*Exhibit A*: Manola with a fan on a page of a ledger book: *Junio, Julio, Agosto.* Column headings for *Recaudación Mensual, Anticipo, Totales,* and *Observaciones* can be seen behind her; and through her fan, figures: *2.50, 2.50, 5, .63, 2.50.*

*Exhibit B*: The postcard marking my place in the Picasso book bears the postmark *Barcelona* and shows a fisheye view of a stone courtyard. Potted ferns and a lace of green spill from windowsills and the balcony. On it Ren's handwriting provides the intelligence that *Here people don't even say they're queer (or whatever)—they say ¿You understand? I feel like I've gone back in time.*

*Testimony*: Dave, graphic designer at my copy shop, is, I discover, a painter. He is represented by a gallery and teaches painting to a class of adult ed. students. *We were on our way from Madrid to Florence so we stopped in Barcelona. The city is old, with a lot of parks,* he says. *The parks were full of life—musicians, and people eating. I did some drawings. We walked around for hours to find the Picasso museum. The city was small enough so that it felt like we walked all over it in just that one day.*

*Corroborating testimony*: Coni, a stylish advertising consultant and witness for the condo association in a case about arrearages on two of the units, visits Barcelona every year. She and her husband plan to retire there.

*Hearsay, excluded*: David Byrne tells an interviewer that his red backpack got stolen in Barcelona.

*Query*: wasn't that Barcelona in Almodóvar's *All About My Mother*?

*Argument:* Barcelona existed in 1900, 1996, 1997, 1980–2000, and 1998. Q.E.D. It is therefore fair to extrapolate its existence in the intervening years and to conclude that Barcelona continues to exist in the twenty-first century.

*Finding, Ruling & Order*: More likely than not it may be, but the burden of proof is by clear and convincing evidence. A view must be taken.

# THE FARAWAY NEARBY

I could live in the next life
if only I could get to it

Driving onto the promontory
again and again, I visit the screened porch

sleep in new-washed sheets
drink the breeze

and depart across the grilled
pause in the road

that is the bridge.  I look quickly
to left or right—is it high

or low tide?  when will
I return to swim in it?

instead of bathing
in my sweat, laboring

to get here.  I mean,
to get *there* for I remain

mired in the city of tasks,
always something urgent

presented unexpectedly
at the very moment of departure.

Oh, the summer of voices, the presence
of the grass, the suggestion

of wings in the moving
leaves as I leave—over

and over again—when I long
to arrive and stay.

# SOME TAX ASPECTS OF LIFE

And a little about
the other of the two certainties.
This is the one that
has us re-living our lives,
year by year, as we
review our annotated
calendars, seemingly
to reprise the numbers,
but in the process
reliving the events
from winter through
the shortest days of the year
preceding the April
of the return.

And at those
innumerable conferences
the Internal Revenue
Code and regs. acquire,
if not personality,
a certain cumbrous
world view
as a speaker suggests
that *The moon
is the perfect environment
for records retention*
or another jokes
that conferees might have
*engaged in prohibited
transactions* with
their secretaries.

Yet the interlaced
numbers and schedules
are only rules, after
all, and, like
other leashes, may
be slipped. That is
why I am standing
here, barefoot, after
dark, beneath faintly coppery

skyglow, on the putting green
of Hole 4 of the
Paradise Resort
golf course, on the
densest, most vibrant,
springiest green I have
ever felt through
my most grateful
surface. I am
engaged
in a prohibited transaction
with the grass.

# CELEBRITY

Interested eyes follow
my every move. I like it,
even as I head for privacy.
And, yes, I sing
into the listening.
              The attentive
hush of the right ears
makes my day, just as
the flash of paparazzi
mars it.
           To be heeded
and loved for my song
is one thing, to be
observed and reported, another.

What my voice delivers
is my soul. The clouds
mention my name.

Part of my triumphant crescendo
is a simple *Forget it* motif
addressed to my rivals,
but I never listen to them
anyhow and equally they
keep out of earshot.

Life is song, a day
the simple pleasures of the park;
danger averted, adoration,
the shared private feast.

What more of heaven could there be
than wind through the dark,
a dapple of lighting from
the moving leaves, and
my heartfelt song?
I trill and lilt
as I tighten my claws on the branch.

# R$_X$

For this bunion,
a liniment.
Faintly oily, mildly
astringent; it contains
witch hazel, a touch
of oil of cloves, and
other ingredients.
Rub it in
at bedtime.
         First
it will soothe
the skin reddened
by stretching.  Then
you will feel
a cooling heat.
         It will
soak through
the skin and penetrate
the bony mass,
gradually reducing
it.
    It will discourage
new growth of
this knob
that robs
substance
from the intricate
fan of the bones of
your foot.
         Each night
rub it in, let it
do its work
during the night.

You will feel it begin to
lessen the tingling pain,
you will feel it
counteract bony accretion
in the lump.

Before the moon
waxes and wanes
three times,
         it will
begin to wane.

# INTERIOR WITH CAT

I look out to the Blue Hills
A scarf of fog drapes the Neponset
On the ladder the cat sharpens
Morning, morning again

Dreams of an oval rug, two chairs
A basement dungeon where on command—
the word *Fash!*—then we must
trade shoes. Prison: our feet hurt

There was a stair up and out—
one could escape but be shot
by the guard crossing the yard
One could be shot. Or in the river, lost

I have escaped into the morn
into the light, light with caws
into the light, light with chirps
Awakening, see: Here is the cat

Stretched out, he is alert,
flat on the deck, awaiting birds
Now I lie back, cool sheets
Listening, washed in the wind

This is today, I have work
It will be hot, I have work
Last night the moon was moist
The train rushes off to the west

The cat chimes once, now the birds
speak with the breeze. A dog *bark-barks*
and with his tail the cat inscribes
curves on the fresh-washed air

Emitters of smoke and noise
become neighbors watering their gardens
I water my garden too, and the cat,
still dry, hurries away

The traffic hastens, the traffic thickens
In the oven my oat bran circles
The cat is chiming, chiming fourteen
And the hands of the clock circle like bone

# FERNANDE

You put your pen down
on the paper and
you looked at me
I looked at you
Then you began to sketch

You drew a breast,
a shoulder, an outline
that was something
like me, but only
something

In your drawings
I looked in vain
for my perfume—*Smoke*
or *Cypress*—you were,
at first, so fluent
that I thought you
could

There are so many
drawings—the one
of me sewing, with
the two positions
of my hand, both drawn

But it is here,
to this one, that
I return. I keep it
by my sewing basket,
on the shelf.

The more you drew—
the thick wrists and ankles
the heavy features
the bull neck—
the more I was effaced

I look at this drawing
now and what I see
is that uncharacteristic

pause—Usually
your pen danced
                and skimmed
the page, but this once
your first move
was to pause
and as you paused
and then looked up
and we exchanged that
look,
          the ink pooled
like a bruise or the heart
that you couldn't see

# LANDSCAPE

To furnish a world,
trees, and a river

Now the trees inscribe
the days in leaves
and we see them, massed,
the forms.  Then the stems
part with the branch and
they release the endlessly
various veined and colored
drawings-out, watercolored.
                              The wind
                  distributes them,
            and the river
with its inscrutable
            currents
bears the nouns away
      taking some
into the lapidary darkness
of its mud(s).

      As the river
                  flows downhill, we could
say that it is constantly
evaluating the gradient
      But it
                  is not
It is thoughtless
It falls, always

giving itself to gravity

In the flats, its trickles
            through marsh
      go down or
they   do   not   go   they spread

Where there is nearly
no down,  they reach                    outward to the edge of the level
where there is a drop

                              and
                         they
                    drop
              with
         it


The river expresses *and*
and *or* better than
anything else—it is
glassy, frothy, thin,
dark, bright, icy, rippled,
and

                              long
(how perfectly the river circumvents
man's volitional mistake)

# DESIDERATUM

The hedge retreated from the house,
every night bivouacking farther from it.
Buildings in its path fell, pavement
was overturned to expose black earth,
and in its wake, the great green
lawn covered this entire sector
of the map.
                    Between the upright
stems of the boxwood—we might as well
call them trunks—there was space
and bare packed dirt, and it seemed as though
creatures of chance might be met there
in the twilight imposed by the dense foliage
of the box.
                    On the lawn, glare
resided, so retreat to the innards
of the hedge was often desirable.

Whatever house the hedge surrounded,
which might have provisioned
the traveler with a cheese and a loaf
to put in the leathern wallet,
was so far distant now that it
was no longer part of the fortune.

It was here in the hedge that
that was now to be sought.

Water was needed, water.
Waiting . . . .
                    In the stir
of leaves in the wind, can be heard
the song of water.

(3)

# THE VOICES

Now that we know
planes are guidable bombs
how like cardboard flesh is

we still hear the voices
from Flight 11 *I see water*
      *and buildings. Oh my God! Oh my God!*
from the 105th floor *We're fucking dying*
from the cockpit
*Get out of here  You can't*
          *come in here*
from airspace over Pennsylvania,
Burnett *I know we're going to die*
*Three of us are going to try to*
        *do something about this*

The messenger who took packages
to Morgan Stanley *There was a woman*
     *there named Ms. Hernandez, who signed*
     *for my packages every day*
     *I don't know if she made it or not, but*
     *I thought about her all night*

The editor of the *Arab American*
*I hate assumption and I hate predictions,*
     *but assume he's an Arab.*
     *I have one request.*
     *Let me kill him.  I would be*
     *satisfied if I kill him personally*

The teacher recalling the day the class talked about
their parents' work and the child who said,
     *My father flies planes into buildings*

the quote from bin Laden
the next morning
that he *admired* what was done

Dubya adlibbing in a prepared speech
*Wanted, Dead or Alive*

from the ruins *Good boy, Porkchop!*
from the stadium, James Earl Jones
*This is not an attack just on*
*the city of New York or*
*the United States of America,*
*but on the very idea of a free,*
*inclusive and civil society*

Keillor on the radio *It is not*
*pleasing to God to rain down destruction*
*from the skies*

from Mohamed Atta's luggage
*Oh, God, open all doors for me.*

from the lunatic
*Save yourselves!  Save the Sears Tower!*

And today, in a letter to the editor
a Muslim reader writes
*Our holybook, the Qur'an, teaches*
If anyone kills an innocent person,
it is as if he has killed all of humanity,
and if anyone saves a life,
it is as if he has saved all of humanity.
*The Arabic word* Islam *comes*
*from the word* salam
*which means* peace.

# MOPPING UP

Sisyphus had a rock
larger than he was,
but I have just
this paper towel
to wipe off the stove.
Sunday, and
millions of others
are mopping up
the world with a paper
towel, or an old rag,
or the corner of their apron
or a brush of their hands.
It doesn't get it tidy—
not completely, or clean—
but it gives a space
to cook, to eat.  And
besides, it's our job.
Here I am again, wiping up
something somebody spilled.
Who spilled it?
There's nobody here but me.

*You must wait till the last minute*
*and always play the black.*
　　　　—One character instructs another
　　　　in "Roulette," a poem by
　　　　Christopher Jane Corkery.

# DIRECTIONS

It is hard to tell
the last minute
from any other, though
if you reach the bridge
over the railroad tracks
you will know that
you've gone too far.
And as for black,
even there there are
shades and degrees—though not,
of course, in relation to
red.
　　　This morning, now,
several blocks away, the boxcars
jostle the air, and what
had been black
is melting into
day

# VOCABULARY

**Cat:** Two large luminous eyes, stripes, and an ever-active tail.

**Cooking:** Playing with your food to make it more interesting.

**Day:** A broad expanse.

**Food:** Still-life material taken by the cook.

**Literature:** A way to live many lives.

**Moment:** All we have.

**Morning:** Opening again.

**Night:** A place of rest, dreams, and renewal.

**Our dead:** Present to us, though physically absent.

**Poetry:** From the darkness, a reaching out toward the light.

**Reading:** Experience on pages.

**Terrorized:** What the passengers of Flight 93 refused to be.

**Thanksgiving:** I have my ticket.

**Work:** A necessary substance.

# PARTICLES

The darkness is lit
by the ambient light of streetlights
the casuistical light of the stars
and the inner light of the mind
      so it is still fairly dark
It is threaded by the distant noise
of planes arriving and departing
the expansive shudder of a bus
and the small snore of a cat

Though these words pass
through me like water
the night is innocent of language

Now the jets are basso continuo
and I can nearly see the page
so I know that dawn is coming on
Hunger mutters under my ribs
              A car passes by
Soon day will claim her attendants
and hold court in city and open air
The Navajo spoken in my dreams
will puzzle the bureaucracy
           of the daytime mind
Look—The cat lifts his head regally
and gives audience to the crows'
announcements of weather and doom
The perpetrator or poet
      (code name *the*) goes
back to sleep

# WE DID

I got lost and ended up taking
somebody else's trip to Maine
There was the dance floor
where she learned to dance—
it was raked (and had linoleum tiles)
There were the Mexican jumping beans
stuck between the pp. of a book
There was the liver-colored spaniel,
the painting of the summerhouse
across the bay, the hot springs
in the cold river (in Maine?)
and the industrial park
where the locals trysted
And I mustn't forget
the reunion where she sat
between two people who were
terrified to see each other again
And the room where we pushed
the twin beds together, she and I

# MEMOIR

I slept in sections—
like cloves of a shallot
Darkness the strong
papery skin holding them

I woke in angles
like planes of a crystal
Light the blindness
binding them cold and solid

I ate in ovoids
like tears of matter
flesh white golden
within my shell

I drank in ribbons
like braids of glitter
my slope the slipping
of spring to pond

I breathed in flowers
like wings of number
their lives the curves
of endless time

I saved in kernels
like gems of hours
secret in folds that
fanned and declined

I gave in rivers
of greengold litanies
their names a slender
cantata of rain

# THE ISLAND

Despite the air of
work in progress—
the blinds up, the table set,
the steady regard of the cat,
the words left on the piece of paper,
the clubbable group of chairs—
the only breathing is the wind's
and, flowing down the back stairs,
the cat's

# HOUSEWORK

Order, too, is a work of art
demanding consummate devotion
To arrange things so that each
seems at home where it is
is a matter of orchestrating
color and shapes with the paths
of our progress through
the rooms. A long gaze
at each thing and a series
of adjustments until it seems
unstudied. Each occasion
of dusting or sweeping
refines the whole:

The windows, cleaned, gather light;
the curtains (ivory gathers) warm and diffuse it;
the lamps, multicolored, save and
release it into evenings in which
the shapes— octagon table, bugle
vase, peacock plate—converse
in a familiar murmur. And though
their words are in the old-world
language that you never learned,
their tones comfort with the feeling
that the speakers will take care
of what needs to be done, will
care for you.

# ACKNOWLEDGMENTS

My thanks to the editors of *The Women's Review of Books*, where "We Did" first appeared, and to the editors of *Kalliope*, where "Serving Two Cats" appeared (both in earlier versions). "The Faraway Nearby" is reprinted by permission from *The Hudson Review*, Vol. LX, No. 4 (Winter 2008), copyright © 2008 by Paula Bonnell.

In the visible world, I am grateful to many who, in ways both concrete and mysterious, enabled me to write and publish this book: Kristin Anderson, the late Diane Bradley (1951-2001), Andrew Giles Buckley, Sharon B. Burke, Joan Carlson, Timothy Q. Cleavenger, Mick Cusimano, Mary Beth DeWalt, Emily G. Fayen, Gwen M. Fournier, Celia Gilbert, Norren Jender, Joanne Kollin Feierman, Arthur Hagadus, Katja Lachner, the late Daniel H. Kelleher (1940-1999), Rebecca Killigrew, Coni and John Martucci, Marnie Mueller, David Penna, Sarah Sutro, the librarians of the Lower Mills branch of the Boston Public Library, my sisters Christine A. Wolfe and Mary J. Wolfe, fellow denizens of the book-and-music-filled 141 Clarion Street; my musical father, the late Dermot F. Wolfe (1914-2004); and my first and most exacting critic, my sister Eileen M. Wolfe. I am also thankful to the Brewer family and the Walker Brothers for renting us a house so conducive to writing and art making, and to my fellow writers and Duxbury-house companions Ruth Butler, Judith Beth Cohen, Christopher Jane Corkery, Sandy Dorr, Alison Eskow, Erica Funkhouser, Laura Gamache, Margo Lockwood, Mary Mitchell, Tema Nason, Susan Quinn, Sue Standing, and Marjorie Waters.

In the invisible world in which readers and writers encounter and evaluate work on the page, I am thankful for the animation of this work by the sensibilities of readers and writers without whom it could not be the book in your hands. I am grateful to the editorial readers for the Ciardi Prize and BkMk Press who sent my manuscript on for further consideration, to poet and critic Mark Jarman who chose it, to my wise and cordial editor Ben Furnish, to Michelle Boisseau for the poetic intelligence of her editorial response to the manuscript, to the intuitive Susan L. Schurman, and for the grace and benevolence of those strangers-to-me-in-person to whom I sent sample poems and asked if they would be willing to look at the manuscript, possibly to give a quote. Naturally I chose writers I admire, respect, and with whom I felt some kinship. Yet I cannot help but be thankful that they saw in this book something they wished to share with you, O reader.

All deficiencies in *Airs & Voices* must be charged to me.

# NOTES

"Words of a Man Who Made His Name": That James King (1864-1933), the grandfather of Martin Luther King, Jr., acquired his surname directly or indirectly from a slaveholder with that name is an assumption of the poem.

"Elegy for an Unlikeable Sister-in-Law": The likeable muse of this poem is a friend in whose voice I hear the last line.

"In Königsberg": When I look up from an early draft, sometimes I say, "Where did *that* come from?" For this, there was a confluence of sources: a description of the logic puzzle known as the Königsberg bridge problem in Simon Singh's book *Fermat's Enigma*, a speech given by Justice Stephen Breyer in which he quoted a judge from India who said he coped with the stress of the courtroom "by going up and hovering near the ceiling. If the case is sufficiently troubling, I go out the window and hover over the city." A friend saying "We'll jump off that bridge when we come to it." And another hard-to-solve problem. Somewhere in the background is the perennial inspiration of the Gordian knot.

"Skywriting": NOPP drifters are devices that measure ocean-current dynamics. *NOPP* being an acronym for the National Oceanographic Partnership Program. Here, for the sake of rhythm and sound, the drifters are called "NOPPs."

"Weather Report": When I was in college, Karl Shapiro visited the campus and talked with students. Under the slanted ceilings of the literary magazine's attic quarters in a building where English literature courses met, he challenged us to write a poem composed of punctuation. It couldn't be done, he said, yet it was clear that the idea appealed to him. It took years before my first response to his challenge was written, years more before this second response surfaced.

"History & a House": Inspired by a passage in Mark Doty's *Heaven's Coast*.

"The Faraway Nearby": The title is from Georgia O'Keeffe.

"Celebrity": Reading two articles—one describing scientists' conclusions about canaries' song, the other a "35 Years Ago" item in the *Boston Phoenix* recounting how Paul McCartney planned to give an impromptu concert in one of the parks in Cambridge but decided not to when the media learned of his intention—somehow gave rise to this.

"Fernande": Was inspired by a talk with slides given by John Richardson at the Museum of Fine Art in Boston and by passages in the first volume of his life of Picasso.

"Directions": Christopher Jane Corkery's *Blessing* is, alas, out of print.

While a practicing lawyer, Paula Bonnell began publishing poems in such places as *Southern Poetry Review, Manhattan Poetry Review,* and *Rattle.* Her first collection, *Message,* includes "Eurydice," a sequence chosen by Albert Goldbarth for a *Poet Lore* narrative-poetry prize, and "Midwest," read by Garrison Keillor on *The Writer's Almanac.* Her essays and book reviews have appeared in such publications as *The Philadelphia Inquirer, The Christian Science Monitor, Boston Review,* and *The New York Times Book Review.* Her awards include poetry prizes from *Negative Capability, Kalliope,* and the Chester H. Jones Foundation, as well as an NEA/PEN Syndicated Fiction prize, and selection by PEN New England as a Discovery writer. A native of western Pennsylvania who has lived in Minnesota, New York, Texas, and Massachusetts, she now makes Boston her home.